insight text guide

Sue Tweg

A Man for All Seasons

Robert Bolt

First published in 2006. Reprinted in 2008, 2012, 2016, 2017, 2018, 2019, 2020.

Insight Publications Pty Ltd
3/350 Charman Road
Cheltenham VIC 3192
Australia
Tel: +61 3 8571 4950
Fax: +61 3 8571 0257
Email: books@insightpublications.com.au

www.insightpublications.com.au

National Library of Australia Cataloguing-in-Publication entry:
Tweg, Sue.
Robert Bolt's A Man for All Seasons: text guide.
For secondary school students.
ISBN 9781921088629.
1. Bolt, Robert, 1924–. A Man for All Seasons. I. Title.
822.914

Other ISBNs:
9781922525130 (digital)
9781922525147 (bundle: print + digital)

Cover design by Gisela Beer, based on a concept by The Modern Art Production Group

Printed in Australia by Ligare

contents

Character map	iv
Introduction	1
Background & context	3
Genre, structure & style	9
Scene-by-scene analysis	15
Characters & relationships	33
Themes, ideas & values	46
Different interpretations	61
Questions & answers	63
Sample answer	66
References & reading	68

CHARACTER MAP

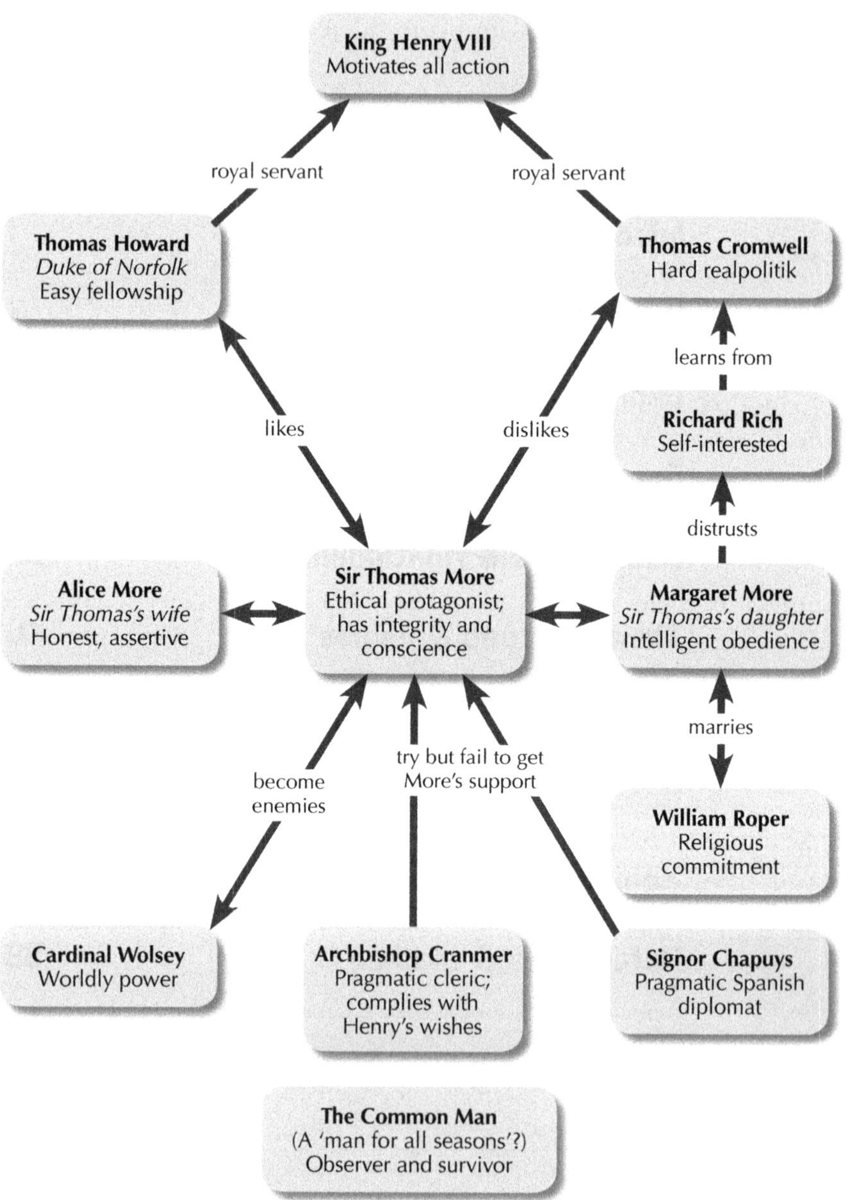

INTRODUCTION

Why write a play about Sir *and* Saint Thomas More, a Tudor lawyer who had his portrait painted by Hans Holbein in 1526 and his head chopped off by order of Henry VIII in 1535? In real life More was a conservative public servant of high principles and formidable intelligence, whose execution for treason led to his enduring fame. He was also a prolific writer, best known for *Utopia* (1516), a book describing an imaginary 'ideal' state. More's contemporary, the Oxford scholar Robert Whittinton, first described him as 'a man for all seasons' (see the two epigraphs to the play). Many others admired and respected him for his integrity, scholarship and humour, among them his friend the great European humanist Erasmus and his ideological opponent at Court, Secretary Thomas Cromwell.

It takes courage, at any time, to stand up against officially sanctioned bullying for what your conscience holds to be right, especially when bullies control the legal system and the state religion. More was not a willing martyr; he used all his lawyer's skills to fight for his life, ultimately relying on the sanctity and letter of the law to protect him.

For Robert Bolt, 'wit' (a medieval word meaning cleverness) to defend personal spiritual integrity is what gives energy to the play's debate about an innocent man whose last words urged others to 'pray to God to give the King good counsel, protesting that he died his faithful servant, and God's first' (*Paris Newsletter* account of More's trial, 1535). As Bolt explains in the play's Preface, what drew him to More's predicament was not so much the unique historical and religious circumstances as 'a hero of selfhood' who would not lie on oath even to save his life (p.xiv).

A Man for All Seasons makes lively, challenging theatre, full of strong characters and More's own clever words. Paul Scofield (who played More onstage and in the 1966 film version) commented:

> The character is so diverse ... Robert Bolt's writing gave me so many clues. It would have been sheer nonsense to re-create some kind of great historical epic; the very act of scaling down the action made the personal tragedy and the human sacrifice so great. (*Radio Times*, BBC, London, 1976)

Most importantly, the play raises crucial political and moral questions that we still face in society today. You don't have to agree with More's religious views to understand why he was condemned or to engage in the same basic arguments. The play encourages debate about our own ideals – would we be prepared to stand up for them, even if it became unsafe? We see old laws safeguarding human rights being altered or even cancelled to meet what politicians worldwide claim to be urgent needs of state. More's life as a subject continues to reflect a testing time for people of good conscience everywhere.

BACKGROUND & CONTEXT

To understand why Henry VIII's public servants and churchmen were inclined in general to go along with his demands and why so much pressure was exerted on More to conform, you need to be aware of the broad historical circumstances affecting England and Europe at the time.

Early Tudor England

The political and religious situations at the end of the fifteenth century when More was born were interconnected and highly unstable. He was about seven in 1485 when the so-called Wars of the Roses (a dynastic struggle between two branches of the same ruling family that caused thirty years of civil war) ended with the death of Richard III on a battlefield. The victor, Henry Tudor, was proclaimed Henry VII; he had to spend the next twenty-four years strengthening his tenuous but defensible claim to the English throne and establishing his own dynasty.

Bolt's Preface sketches in the next historical step. Henry's heir, Prince Arthur (a clever choice of name to gain popularity by evoking the heroic tradition of King Arthur), died soon after his marriage in 1501 to Catherine, Princess of Aragon. The second son, Prince Henry, married Arthur's widow (principally to maintain the Spanish alliance) and was crowned Henry VIII in 1509. In order to marry his brother's wife, normally a forbidden relationship in Christian church law, Henry was given a special dispensation by Pope Julius II.

The rise of public servants

Another significant development was occurring at this time in power relations around the monarch. Feudal aristocrats who fought for power during the Wars of the Roses were beginning to lose ground to a new breed of career public servants. Henry VIII still surrounded himself with hereditary nobility, like More's friend the Duke of Norfolk, but astute commoners were also rising through the ranks of public office. These included Thomas Cromwell, a farrier's son who became Henry's Secretary of State, then Chancellor; and Richard Rich, who rose through positions in the legislature to become Lord Chancellor in his turn. Henry's most influential chancellor, Thomas Wolsey, was a butcher's son who became a cardinal.

Thomas Cromwell

Cromwell, especially, exerted control over parliamentary business by lobbying and drafting Bills, and supervised affairs of the Church in the interests of good management for the Crown. Unlike Wolsey, who rose to power through the Church, Cromwell was a layman and a pragmatist, a man to do the King's business. He devised constitutional ways to both limit the independent power of bishops and, more significantly, redirect the prime allegiance of English clergy to the monarch rather than the pope. He also supervised the wholesale closure of monasteries in England, appropriating the Roman Catholic Church's considerable wealth for Henry's treasury.

While More expressed his own views on religious reform, he did so from a conservative position within the faith and was opposed to Cromwell's idea of supreme control of English Catholics by the English king.

The Reformation

To appreciate More's dilemma you need to consider how he would have been reacting to religious changes of the period. It isn't necessary to understand all the details of the Reformation as it affected England (specifically from 1529 to 1559) to follow the play's arguments and points of religious tension. Read Dickens (1964) for more information about this period of history; and see Bolt's discussion in the Preface of how he draws on history to create a drama about 'the way it was lived' (p.x).

Catholicism in England and Europe

Early Tudor England was part of a larger European 'unity' of Christian countries (France, Germany, Spain, Italy and Austria), supposedly held together by spiritual allegiance to the supreme head of the Roman Catholic Church, the Pope. Generations of disgracefully mercenary popes and rival popes, as well as a few good ones, had been tolerated by English people who had gone on practising their Christian religion at a mostly untroubled distance from European scandals.

There had been earlier English critics of the Papacy and Catholic beliefs and practices, like John Wycliffe (d.1384), whose followers were intermittently persecuted and derisively named 'Lollards' (mumblers of prayers). The influence of Lollardy was low-profile but persistent and widespread, stimulating social and political debate about the place of religion in everyday life. Specific targets, like Cardinal Wolsey, the Papal Legate and Chancellor of England, fuelled criticism of the Church.

Thomas More, who succeeded Wolsey, was the first non-clerical Chancellor for generations, yet he was a pious, conservative Catholic who hated heretics (people who thought, spoke and wrote about things contrary to authorised Catholic doctrine). More was authorised to read and report on heretical writings in England and when he became Lord Chancellor he was proud to describe himself as 'relentless towards thieves, murderers and heretics' (written as his own epitaph).

Luther

Criticism of the established Church became more focused in Europe after 1517, when Martin Luther, a monk and professor of theology at the University of Wittenberg, began a series of public attacks on corrupt Church practices. His writings were widely spread, causing violent debate across Europe. This lengthy religious and cultural upheaval, known as the Reformation, devastated individuals on all sides and split countries along religious lines.

Eventually, the European 'Roman' Catholic tradition, maintaining allegiance to the Pope as spiritual head of a country's religious life, was divided from the 'Protestantism' of countries that no longer recognised the supreme authority of a pope. In the play, Roper exemplifies the shifting thoughts of the time when he argues passionately both for and against Luther's reforming ideas (p.17, p.36).

The royal divorce

Bolt's 'Common Man' suggests that in England, the Reformation 'was achieved not by bloodshed but by simple Act of Parliament' (p.47). The catalyst for change was Henry VIII's divorce and remarriage which, as the play shows, had serious political as well as religious consequences – and blood was certainly shed in the process. It brought down Cardinal Wolsey, enhanced Cromwell's control and trapped More in a fatal dilemma.

After eighteen years of marriage failed to produce a living male heir, Henry moved to divorce Catherine of Aragon and marry Anne Boleyn for 'reasons of state'. Divorce required the Pope to reverse the original papal dispensation of 1509 (agreed on theological grounds) to invalidate the royal marriage in 1527 (on contrary theological grounds).

The play picks up the controversy in two important scenes: firstly when Wolsey tries to win More's support (pp.10–13), and secondly when Henry tries to bully More (pp.29–34). The crux of the argument for conscientious Catholics was a conflict between irreconcilable passages in the Bible about marrying a brother's wife. In the end the new Archbishop of Canterbury, Thomas Cranmer, supported Henry and declared the royal marriage null and void. Cromwell then pushed legislation through Parliament to enforce compliance with Henry's will.

In the play, Henry appeals to More to help him clear his 'conscience' for making an incestuous marriage with Catherine. His textual authority is Leviticus 18:16, 'Thou shalt not uncover the nakedness of thy brother's wife', a point reiterated in Leviticus 20:21, 'if a man take his brother's wife, it is an unclean thing ... they shall be childless'. More, in reply, cites Deuteronomy 25:5, which appears to support the idea of marrying a dead brother's wife.

Three Bills guided through Parliament by Cromwell to become new statutes between 1532 and 1534 compromised More's beliefs and loyalties; in his view, the legitimate moral and spiritual power of the Church was undermined permanently for political expediency – that is, simply to allow Henry's divorce to proceed.

Submission of the clergy

This was a process which made the Convocation (assembly of bishops) forbidden to legislate except by licence and assent of the Crown. More resigned the Chancellorship in protest (see p.48, pp.52–3).

Succession Act

After Archbishop Cranmer declared the marriage to Catherine null and void, Parliament recognised Henry's marriage to Anne Boleyn and settled royal succession on their children as legitimate heirs. Slandering the marriage was treason; compliance was required by an oath. The play emphasises the significance of this Act in More's concern about the actual wording of the oath (pp.73–4), his interrogation after he refuses to take it (pp.76–9), and the way in which Margaret compromises herself by trying to persuade him to save his life (p.83).

Act of Supremacy

In 1521 Henry wrote a book defending the papacy and refuting Luther's arguments about Catholic sacraments, for which Pope Leo X granted him the title *Fidei Defensor*, Defender of the Faith. The abbreviation FID DEF is still found near the sovereign's head on all English coins. Henry was excommunicated in 1533 by Pope Clement VII. In a final retaliation, the 1534 Act unequivocally declared the King to be Supreme Head of the English Church, rejecting all foreign authority (i.e. the Pope) in ecclesiastical matters.

More: a virtuous career in the world

More struggled inwardly to balance two ways of being, the spiritual and the worldly. He was rigorously pious, attending daily services in his private chapel and secretly wearing a hair shirt throughout his life to mortify the flesh. At the same time, he was a successful lawyer, royal servant and head of a large family household in Chelsea. The play illustrates both aspects of More's character, especially during the scene in which Henry makes a 'surprise' visit (pp.25–41).

Utopia

More was associated with the foremost European thinkers and scholars of the time. Today he might be called a 'public intellectual', although he was not given to public pronouncements so much as known for his devotional writings and *Utopia*, an expression of More's ideas for a perfectly organised civil society.

Argument and wit

The intellectual energy that characterised More's relationships can be traced in several ways in Bolt's play. Consider how he engages in argument with two very different young men, Rich (e.g. pp.2–5) and Roper (e.g. pp.16–18). He exercises his wit with Wolsey, Cromwell, Chapuys, Norfolk, Henry, Cranmer, Alice and Margaret. More's Christian humanist approach to education for women is exemplified in the affectionate pride he has in his daughter Margaret's erudition, and in his offer to teach Alice to read.

'The English Socrates'

A sinister note on More's political situation is introduced by Chapuys, who reminds More that Erasmus calls him 'the English Socrates' (p.49). This is a dangerously attractive nickname for someone who is tempted to face the prospect of martyrdom for his principles. More is well aware that Socrates, condemned for expressing critical ideas on ethics and politics in the Greek state, could have escaped but chose bravely to accept a cup of hemlock as a death sentence in 399 BC.

GENRE, STRUCTURE & STYLE

Genre

Bolt explores More's life crisis in a dramatised debate between all the historical figures who were part of More's circle of family, friends and political colleagues. Think of the play as a lively integration of two powerful dramatic genres: the morality play and Brecht's 'epic theatre'. Each of these forms has an acknowledged philosophical and didactic (teaching) purpose.

Morality play

The morality play was a Tudor genre evolving from medieval mystery play cycles. It was intended to pack a moral punch and get the Christian audience thinking about the state of their souls. Best known and still performed is *Everyman* (c.1495), a powerful dramatisation of the worldly protagonist's surprise encounter with Death personified. Appropriately named to indicate that he represents everybody, 'Everyman' panics as his relatives, his drinking mate 'Fellowship' and then his worldly possessions (all personified as comic characters) refuse to go on the journey with him – In the end each soul must be alone.

Bolt's play follows the *Everyman* pattern of didactic episodes showing moral evolution. The morality play core is evident in More's key speech about the Seven Deadly Sins, Virtues and human choice (pp.83–4) and in his execution scene (pp.98–9). Think about each character More encounters as either a challenge to him or a support – what does each one contribute to his awareness of the journey? Then read More's own words in the speech after he has been accused of High Treason, 'Death ... comes for us all, my lords ... their success is uncertain' (pp.90–1).

Epic theatre

The Common Man with his props basket and habit of addressing the audience immediately signals a modern form of anti-naturalistic political theatre evolved by Bertolt Brecht in Germany between the two World Wars and made famous by the Berliner Ensemble after 1949. Brecht's 'epic theatre' aims to be a secular morality play, turning the complacent spectator into an alert observer who studies what's going on and makes decisions about an issue being depicted. There's no neat conclusion, but rather an open-ended questioning for the audience. Epic theatre is discussed further under Style below.

More's theatrical metaphors

It's appropriate that Bolt chose drama for this subject matter because More himself frequently used theatrical metaphors in his writing and considered the purpose of humans to be obedient players (whether they liked it or not) in whatever plan God had for the world.

In *Utopia*, Book 1, a conversation occurs between an imaginary student, Raphael, who says 'there's no room at court for philosophy', and More, who answers:

> There's certainly no room for the academic variety ... *But there is a more civilised form of philosophy which knows the dramatic context, so to speak, tries to fit in with it, and plays an appropriate part in the current performance.* That's the sort you should go in for ... *do the best you can to make the present production a success – don't spoil the whole play just because you happen to think of another one that you'd enjoy rather more ... The same rule applies to politics and life at Court.* (trans. Turner, More 1965, p.63; my italics)

Structure

Two acts allow for an interval in performance and suggest a long passage of historical time: Act One covers 1526 to 1530; Act Two begins in 1532 and ends on 6 July 1535. The danger for More increases appreciably by the opening of Act Two.

The play's structure follows 'epic theatre' conventions, using a montage of disparate scenes that highlight key moments of the issue being explored. Bolt divides the action into units which I've numbered Scenes 1–17 with page numbers from the Heinemann edition. A change in location and/or time is signalled simply by lighting (e.g. p.13, p.81) or by making use of the Common Man, who resets the space with basic furniture while he comments on the next situation where he'll be asked to play another 'character' (e.g. pp.9–10, p.57).

Style: epic theatre techniques

The play's style uses a combination of epic theatre presentation and brief realist interactions in the play's world. Bolt intends the Common Man to function as a 'dislocating' element for the audience, which is used to being passively receptive of a story. Use the term 'alienation effect' if you like, because it's well known (even though its meaning is not well understood). However, be aware that 'alienation' in this context does not mean that you are being turned *away* – being alienated – from the arguments in the play; rather, Brecht (and Bolt) wanted audiences to be passionately attentive and *involved* in the questions being debated.

A more accurate translation of the German *Verfremdungseffekt* (*V-effekt*) is 'strange-making effect'. The idea is that audience members should be prevented from being drawn completely into the world of the play and suspending disbelief, by obvious reminders that they are watching a fictional and highly selective 're-creation' onstage. Then the usual emotional pull of 'characters' that typifies realist theatre takes second place to an intelligent focus on issues.

The Common Man, explains Bolt, is 'the most notorious of the alienation devices, an actor who addresses the audience and comments on the action' (Preface, p.xviii). Brecht's aim was to activate the audience's political consciousness so that people would leave the theatre moved by what they had seen and, fired up with ideas about society's wrongs, wanting to do something positive to change things in reality.

The language spoken by all characters is conversational, argumentative, plain-speaking, mostly modern in tone. The text also incorporates phrases from More's writings, reported speeches and phrases, Tudor documents, son-in-law William Roper's *Life of More* and Margaret's letters.

Style: poetic techniques

In Bolt's view 'a play is more like a poem than a straight narration' (Preface, p.xvi). One poetic feature of Bolt's writing is its rich use of imagery. Key images include those of the four elements – water, fire, air and earth – and of the river (the Thames), a symbol of the political fluctuations and divisions throughout the play.

The four elements

Water imagery includes references to the sea, tides, sailing, navigation and ships. Bolt calls the sea 'a figure for the superhuman context ... the largest, most alien, least formulated thing I know' (Preface, p.xvi).

- Explore implications of the following: More is 'easily sea-sick ... [and] afraid of drowning' (p.24); Rich is 'adrift' (p.38); Henry's description of 'respect' (in the abstract) as 'water in the desert' (p.32).

Fire can have both positive and negative associations: it can suggest warmth and light, or punishment. Candles indicate conspiratorial meetings at night (p.11 – Wolsey *'snatches up candle and holds to* MORE's *face'* – and p.41), and the threat of execution – Cranmer will be burned alive in the future (p.75).

- Explore the significance of collecting bracken for the family fire (p.64), and of Rich's hand being held to the flame by Cromwell (p.46).

Air signifies freedom; random or impulsive actions; wind; stormy weather and danger.

- Explore the significance of air imagery in the context of Norfolk's falcon (pp.5–6) and More's view of Roper's 'seagoing principles' (p.39).

Earth suggests the human element; dry land; safety.

- 'Dry land' signifies society for Bolt (Preface, p.xvi).
- Examine More's safe 'thickets of the law' imagery, which brings together all four elements (p.39).

The river

Bolt draws attention to this powerful symbol of the dangerous ebb and flow of More's political world. Significantly, the King calls it '*my* river' (p.27) and is anxious to 'catch the tide' (p.34). The Thames runs through London, connecting More's safe private world (his family house in Chelsea) with public arenas where he must justify himself (Richmond Palace, Westminster Hall, the Tower).

Repetitions and echoes

You'll become aware of similar words and phrases being used by different characters. This is an aspect of Bolt's poetic style that works on the audience subconsciously, inducing a slightly uncomfortable sense that authorised eavesdropping is rampant in More's world – and also that everyone is involved in the unfolding crisis.

- Repeated words suggest a dangerous climate of suspicion, making us wonder who overheard that comment when it was first articulated and why it is being repeated.
- Henry says 'No courtship, no ceremony, Thomas. Be seated' to More (p.30), echoed playfully by Cromwell to Rich (p.42) – that Cromwell dares to mimic the King is indicative of his confidence.
- Cromwell makes a similar show of superiority over Norfolk, with 'this isn't Spain' (p.61) mimicking Norfolk's supposedly private words with More (p.53).

Repetition also works as wry comedy:

- Margaret and More counter each other's intensely serious arguments with the wry 'that's very neat' (p.83).

- The repetition of 'third alternative' comments by Cromwell (p.58) and Chapuys (p.63) link them as equally cunning strategists trying to manage dimwits.
- The Common Man states he can 'feel [his] deafness coming on' (p.80), echoing his earlier 'I'll go deaf blind and dumb' (p.25). Although this is humorous, deafness takes on sinister overtones through the crucial 'deafness' of two essential witnesses in the same small room as More and Rich (p.95).

Repeated words reveal differences in the individuals who use them. See notes in 'Themes, Ideas & Values' on the use of the word 'friend' by Rich, Henry, Norfolk and More; and for discussion of the word 'convenient' used by Margaret, Roper, Cromwell and Rich.

SCENE-BY-SCENE ANALYSIS

Although Bolt did not number individual scenes, these are nevertheless clearly defined through the use of lighting and the Common Man's direct addresses to the audience. Using these structural breaks in the action, I have divided Act One into Scenes 1–7 and Act Two into Scenes 8–17.

ACT ONE (1526 to 1530)

Scene 1 (pp.1–9)

Summary: *The Common Man opens play, becoming the Steward to More's household; More and Rich discuss Cromwell, bribery (silver cup); More summoned to night interview with Wolsey.*

The opening scene establishes the Common Man as scene and props setter, 'presenter' of characters to the audience, and a commentator on, as well as participant in, the action.

It also sets the mood of More's domestic world – a civilised gentleman's home, with a benign master; a place to find hospitality, generosity, good food and drink; friendly disputes with equal sharing of conversation; and genuine family piety (prayers).

Rich, the young lawyer, is awkward in the relaxed family environment from the outset, partly because he needs money and employment, and partly because he envies More's status. In conversation he is philosophically and politically out of tune with his hosts: he admires Cromwell, but the Cromwells clearly do not admire him. He states one of the play's central ideas, that 'every man has his price' (p.2), a notion that Rich endorses but More refutes. More associates the quote with Machiavelli – read the note (p.104) for information on this Italian statesman and political writer.

A series of disruptions increases the tension:

- Norfolk's news of Cromwell's promotion to Wolsey's Secretary (does Rich know already?) unsettles the More family.

- More being sent for by Wolsey so late is worrying; as Alice correctly guesses, it must be related to the sensitive issue of the royal divorce, so is potentially dangerous for the statesmen involved.
- Although Rich gratefully takes the silver cup from More, it leads to his being challenged by Matthew, who thinks Rich has stolen it.

Q Are we encouraged to have any sympathy for Richard Rich?

Q What is the dramatic purpose of the banter between Norfolk and Alice?

Q What does the general undercurrent of interest in Cromwell indicate?

Scene 2 (pp.9–13)

Summary: *More opposes Wolsey's tactics for divorce; they discuss the need for the King to have male heirs; the Common Man takes the role of the Boatman.*

This scene sets Cardinal Wolsey, a secular cleric with a strong grasp of political realities – and anxious about his own security if he fails to facilitate Henry's divorce – against More's immovable religious and ethical values. It's the forerunner of challenging arguments to come for More in scenes with Cromwell, an even more hostile opponent.

Wolsey hopes he can use More's high status among European Catholics to help pressure the Pope for another dispensation for Henry. More uses his wits to handle a dangerous conversation about the Tudor dynasty's weakness unless Henry (with a new wife) has a son. In this matter, More's duty as Councillor of England collides with his private conscience. Wolsey resents More's 'moral squint' (p.10) because it shames his own unscrupulous manipulation of religion. He confronts More with his public duty, using words Henry will later echo: 'your conscience is your own affair; but you're a statesman!' (p.12).

Wolsey's question about who would be a fitting successor to himself (p.13) is intended to alert More to his public responsibility. If More won't take on the dangerous but powerful role of Lord Chancellor, should his friend John Fisher, Bishop of Rochester (high-principled but politically naive) be asked, or would Cromwell immediately seize the opportunity for himself?

Key point

Wolsey says, 'in addition to Prayer there is Effort' (p.11). This is the crux of More's problem – he would like to let God's will be done by just letting prayer work and good things happen.

Q How do you interpret Wolsey's insistence to More that 'we're alone ... There's no one here' (p.11) and what follows immediately after in the conversation?

Q How does More try to maintain his moral position?

Q What makes Wolsey declare himself More's 'enemy' (p.13)?

Scene 3 (pp.13–16)

Summary: *More encounters Cromwell, then Chapuys, the Spanish Ambassador.*

This scene emphasises the dangerous dilemma More faces by reinforcing the division that Henry's divorce is already creating – Cromwell and Chapuys are on opposite sides and each wants More to declare his support for their cause.

Cromwell is especially threatening, signalling that as Wolsey's Secretary he will keep his eye on More. In contrast, Chapuys emphasises his diplomatic status, with the full weight of Spain and the Holy Roman Empire as his authority. Notice how skilfully he suggests that More's guarded response implies support for the Queen's cause (i.e. opposition to the divorce).

Key point

Immediately after these encounters, More observes how 'black' the river looks. Notice the Boatman's reply about the deep channel 'in the middle' (p.16). This is where More, who is no sailor, must attempt to steer his own course in a political sense.

Q Examine the conversation between the Boatman and More – how do they relate? What significant points do you notice, metaphorically as well as literally?

Scene 4 (pp.16–20)

Summary: *More refuses to give Roper permission to marry Margaret; More avoids discussion about the royal divorce and becoming Chancellor; the Common Man describes Wolsey's death.*

We begin to understand that More's dangerous political situation has domestic repercussions, since he strives to keep his personal views secret even from his family. He realises that Wolsey's fall would be catastrophic, using another water metaphor – 'the splash would swamp a few small boats like ours' (pp.19–20) – to suggest the sense of insecurity this would bring about.

More-family dynamics

More is portrayed as a humane witty man who likes Roper for his intelligence but not as a husband for Margaret if he's unsettled spiritually. We're reminded of More's strong professional stand on 'heretics' and his theological conservatism.

There is another brief interlude between More and his daughter Margaret. She has a grasp of the political situation and wants him to share his views, but he warns her not to 'talk treason' (p.18). We learn from Matthew's remarks to Cromwell in the next scene that More would normally discuss problems with her – 'so he's worried' (p.23).

The mood lightens briefly when Alice enters. More jokes about Margaret's expensive education and Alice's 'dangerous, levelling talk' (p.19), trying to deflect the serious danger of discussing politics, even in domestic privacy.

Q How is More's love for his daughter and wife revealed?

Q Find some examples of More's 'wit' in this scene.

Q Why does More think Wolsey's 'fall' would be so devastating?

Scene 5 (pp.20–4)

Summary: *More succeeds Wolsey as Chancellor; Cromwell targets Rich's ambitious streak; Chapuys and Cromwell argue about More's response to the King's divorce; the Steward plays informer.*

The focus shifts from More to the powerful servants of state whose activities shape political outcomes.

Key point

The Common Man quotes an imaginary historian who describes More as a saint with 'wilful indifference to realities' (p.20). The play, however, creates a more complex depiction of More than this, showing his struggle to conquer his fears and stay true to his principles despite being fully aware of the 'realities' motivating others.

Rich's apprenticeship in devious statecraft begins under Cromwell's tutelage. Cromwell plays him like a fish on a hook with hints of a job offer: flustered and trying to guess what answer Cromwell wants to hear, Rich denies having a close friendship with More (compare this with his conversation with More, p.3). This is his first betrayal of More, the benefactor who tried to give him good advice in the opening scene.

This scene suggests that 'intelligence gathering' is an absurd game with serious consequences. Rich is caught in the crossfire of two well-matched experts, Cromwell and Chapuys. Then the Steward, an experienced informant, entertainingly demonstrates how to play his game of telling each side what they want to know without giving much away ... and getting paid for it (pp.23–5).

Q Why is Rich 'furious' with the Steward (p.24)?

Q The Steward reveals an important fuller picture of More to the audience: 'he has rheumatism, prefers red wine to white, is easily sea-sick, fond of kippers, afraid of drowning' (p.24). Why is this kind of information useless to people like Cromwell, but useful to an audience?

Scene 6 (pp.24–41)

Summary: *The King's 'surprise' visit; Henry fails to persuade More to support his divorce, leaves before dinner; Roper and More argue about the law.*

This scene falls into two parts. First, there's the flurry of activity to prepare More for the King's arrival, followed by Henry's showdown with More about the divorce. Second, More argues with Roper about the importance of the law.

In a semi-comic beginning, we see how More's religious devotions take priority even when the King visits. His family tries to rearrange the outer man to look like the Chancellor rather than a priest. More, though, presents himself as he is – no sham, no artifice of 'position' or fake surprise. Compare More's outlook to Henry's appearance *'in cloth of gold'* (p.27) – wilful, domineering, petulant, frustrated and looking for More's flattery and compliance.

Key point

Henry's pilot's whistle is a key prop: he enjoys his power to silence others and make them kneel. More neatly pricks the pompous bubble with his ironic comment on 'fear' for what his 'household can bear' (p.27), but by the time Henry leaves they will begin to feel real fear.

Rich arrives to interrupt the argument brewing between Roper and More and becomes the focus of attention, which he assumes is hostile. Already disloyal and 'adrift' (p.38), Rich makes a final attempt to be accepted by More. More refuses to accept Rich's assurance that he will be 'steadfast': 'Richard, you couldn't answer for yourself even so far as tonight' (p.38). This stinging refusal lays the groundwork for Rich's final act of betrayal.

Rich's exit leads to a fierce argument about English law and the family's safety. At one level, it's about a father's worried refusal to give his daughter to a political hothead. Significantly, too, it reveals More's deep belief in the strength of the law as protection in dangerous times ahead.

Pay close attention to imagery. More speaks imaginatively of the law as trees and thickets in which he, a master forester, can hide. He condemns Roper's zeal to get at the Devil by cutting down laws in a radical 'deforestation'. More then attacks Roper's 'seagoing principles' (p.39), explaining what he means after apologising for speaking so harshly (p.41).

Q How do Henry's words and actions in his interview with More contradict his claim to be 'in an excellent frame of mind' (p.31)?

Q Notice how the dramatic tension changes at eight o'clock when the tide changes – how can this be read metaphorically as well as literally?

Q Look up the meanings of 'the golden calf' and 'Moloch' (p.39): what do Roper and More mean by invoking these ancient idols?

Scene 7 (pp.41–6)

Summary: *The Common Man as the Publican at 'The Loyal Subject' pub; Cromwell explains administrative 'factor of convenience' to Rich; finds out about the silver cup; demonstrates how More can be frightened by pain.*

Comedy shapes the opening of this scene. The Common Man takes on the classic role of a discreetly ignorant publican who sees, hears and knows nothing about his patrons' conspiratorial business. Moreover, he can play up to Cromwell's threats without being intimidated (pp.41–2).

Rich's political progress

Cromwell has set up this meeting specifically to recruit Rich, who demonstrates that Cromwell has offered the right price – a prestigious administrative job – to get him to report on More. Rich would like to think he's just lost his political innocence, but Cromwell knows better (p.44).

Rich learns quickly to equate More's religious scruples with 'administrative inconvenience' (p.44). However, wine and a few shreds of conscience about More galvanise Rich into a final flash of defiance against Cromwell, who has mastered him so effortlessly. 'You wouldn't find [More] easy to frighten!' (p.46), Rich jeers. Cromwell's violence is unexpected but may reflect his exasperation with Rich.

Q Explain why 'The Loyal Subject' is an ironic name for the tavern where this conspiratorial meeting takes place.

Q Why does the Publican make sly remarks about More being too deep for the likes of him?

Q Why does Cromwell respond so violently to Rich's jeering comment?

ACT TWO (1532 to 1535)

Scene 8 (p.47)

Summary: *The Common Man fills in significant details of 1530–32.*

This short scene provides an important grounding for Act Two. The Common Man reads from the work of a 'historian' who assesses the foundation of the Church of England as a relatively benign 'compromise', resisted by 'an unhappy few'. The historian's generalising rhetoric is inadequate for the playwright, whose aim is to explore how that history was lived by individuals like More, his family and his contemporaries (see the Preface, p.x).

Note the imagery used by the Common Man – 'water's flowed under the bridge' – and the historian's phrases 'torrents of religious passion', 'canals of moderation' and 'current of their times'. Remember that Bolt associates water with destructiveness and the unknown 'superhuman context' (Preface, p.xvi). In this passage, water imagery suggests events flowing relatively smoothly, but the play's events show that this period was actually characterised by great uncertainty, anxiety and violence.

Q Why does the Common Man like the way the historian writes?

Q Would you agree that 'we are dealing with an age *less fastidious than our own*' (my emphasis)?

Scene 9 (pp.47–57)

Summary: *More resists Chapuys's temptation to commit treason or accept martyrdom; he resigns the Chancellorship when the Convocation submits; his household is reduced; the Steward leaves.*

This scene is structured as a series of tense encounters for More at a critical moment of waiting for news that will force him to act.

First he's amused by Roper's theatrical demonstration with a cross and black costume. Roper thinks he's being daring to signal 'allegiance' to the Roman Church (hence the wry humour about Spain and heresy), while More waits to see if he'll have to put his conscience to the test in more than a show.

After Chapuys's unwelcome reference to Socrates (a martyr for his ideals) and repellent attempt to make More share his 'brothers in Christ' platitude, More has to contend with the ambassador's real business – incitement to make his resignation a 'signal' for rebellion. More's horrified realisation that his resignation has darker consequences is now interrupted by Roper, Alice, Margaret and Norfolk. This is a key moment onstage as he appeals for help to remove his chain of office.

Key point

More finally has to choose between his public duty and private conscience. He resigns the Chancellorship from a personal ethical and religious position – but it has wider political significance, much more serious than he might have considered, as Chapuys points out (p.51).

More knows it's sinister that Cromwell's man toured the North Country with Chapuys and that Norfolk isn't worried by his warning about possible rebellion. This leaves the audience feeling that a dangerous net is closing around More.

Q Why is it Margaret who helps More remove the chain?

Q Why is the Common Man as 'Matthew' outraged by More's personal farewell?

Scene 10 (pp.57–62)

Summary: *Cromwell tries to set up a bribery charge against More with Rich's assistance but fails; Cromwell recruits Norfolk with a threat; the Common Man becomes Rich's Steward.*

This scene demonstrates Cromwell's methods of neutralising opposition. The audience remembers the silver cup that More gave to Rich in the opening scene; now Cromwell suggests it's 'evidence' of More's corruption. The charge fails when Norfolk – suddenly using real intelligence – recalls the precise date on which Rich was given the cup and realises that More rejected the bribe.

Cromwell's unsubtle threat to Norfolk about the King's wish that he be involved in his friend's investigation to demonstrate there's no 'persecution' immediately alerts us to the actual persecution Cromwell intends to carry out.

Key point

Although Norfolk thinks More's silence is not dangerous, Cromwell already knows that it 'is bellowing up and down Europe!' (p.58). We now realise that More's tactic, spelled out in the previous scene, won't be sufficient to protect him.

Ominously for More, who puts absolute trust in the law, Cromwell tells Rich 'it must be done by law. It's just a matter of finding the right law. Or making one' (p.61).

Q Disconcertingly, Cromwell echoes Norfolk's own words to More (on p.53) back to him: 'This isn't Spain' (p.61). Does this suggest Cromwell has been spying on Norfolk and More? What is the significance of these references to Spain?

Q In what way is Rich just the right 'size' for the Steward to manage as a new master?

Scene 11 (pp.62–6)

Summary: *Domestic impoverishment and tension; More refuses Chapuys's treasonable letter from Spain; summoned to Cromwell to answer charges.*

Chapuys's last visit puts More in even graver danger because he brings a personal letter from the King of Spain, for whom King Henry is 'heretic'. More repeatedly insists from now on that his views cannot be 'known' but only 'guessed at' as long as he keeps silent (p.63).

Domestic decline reflects More's fall from royal favour and the danger of accepting money from bishops, which would be construed as payment for writing a treasonable opinion. The cold house, poor food, lack of servants, the family's constant anxiety and More's deliberate lack of hospitality to Chapuys (p.64) all contrast strongly with the atmosphere in the play's opening scene.

Q Is Chapuys being incautious to visit More with such a treasonable letter, or would it be in Spain's and the Catholic Church's interests to make More a martyr for their cause?

Scene 12 (pp.66–70)

Summary: *Cromwell interrogates More on spurious 'charges'; crisis point.*

The initially civilised conversational tone ('good of you to come', p.66) rapidly deteriorates. More uses 'wit' as his weapon in wry comments about Rich ('we're old friends', p.66), being amazed (p.67), and his awareness of the King's 'generosity' (p.67). The scene's tension develops in incremental steps of 'pressure' from Cromwell:

- first, a flattering offer of the King's favour
- then a charge of treasonable sympathy with the 'Holy Maid of Kent' (More had examined the nun Ann Barton at the King's request; More refutes this charge by evidence of witnesses)

- then Henry's book – despite Cromwell's suggestions, More knows Henry can't accuse More of writing the now treasonable ideas about the authority of the 'Bishop of Rome' (i.e. the Pope) over sacraments (pp.68–9).

Cromwell finally introduces the central issue – the King's remarriage. This leads to the interrogation's climax, in which Cromwell plays his trump card: a direct threat from the King declaring that More is a 'traitorous' subject (p.69). More acknowledges that he is 'brought here at last' (p.69) – that is, he realises he faces a very serious charge and sentence.

Cromwell's metaphorical summing up – 'There's a man who raises the gale and won't come out of harbour' (p.69) – expresses his irritation that More won't break his silence and fight. More disturbs Cromwell because he makes unusual trouble, difficult for a state servant to understand and conquer.

Q More earlier dismissed lawyer Cromwell as a 'pragmatist' (i.e. just a workman lawyer going for results, not a smart legal scholar like himself) and thought of his own case as 'watertight' (p.66). Might his views have changed after this confrontation?

Q Why do you think Rich is '*subdued*' (p.70) by Cromwell's explanation of how Henry will want to justify More's destruction?

Scene 13 (pp.70–4)

Summary: *More stages a quarrel with Norfolk to drive his friend away and stay true to himself; Roper and Margaret tell him about the Act of Succession oath.*

This scene falls into two parts, each with an argument at its centre.

In the first argument, More and Norfolk return to the question of 'self' they argued over briefly in Scene 9 (p.53). This time it's crucial for More to make Norfolk understand how depth of spiritual commitment defines a person of conscience. (For further discussion of these ideas see the 'Themes, Ideas & Values' section.)

In the second argument, More insists on paying close attention to the specific words in the new oath (p.74). As a scholarly lawyer, More has been trained to handle words subtly. His long speech to Roper and Meg is meant to inspire them for the trials to come: 'our natural business lies in escaping' (p.74). For the audience, this reaffirms More's balance of 'wit' and pious obedience to God's plans just before the final test.

Q What does More know will finally catch Norfolk's attention and enrage him enough to leave? (Relate this final reaction to More's comment about Norfolk being able to argue 'like [theologian] Thomas Aquinas over a rat-dog's pedigree', p.72.)

Q Does Roper have more sense of the political urgency of the moment than More?

Scene 14 (pp.74–81)

Summary: *The Common Man becomes the Jailer, informs audience about historical fate of Cromwell, Norfolk, Cranmer and Rich; More is imprisoned, interrogated at night; refuses to submit.*

Through this scene, the audience learns that More did not take the oath and has been imprisoned in the Tower for a year.

A letter from God

The visual humour of the 'letter from God' reminds the audience of several important things at once.

- It produces a Brechtian *V-effekt* to indicate that the world of the play is artificial – so we need to keep our intelligence alert at the very point in Bolt's play where we'll feel most emotionally involved in More's situation. (See 'Style: epic theatre techniques' in the previous section of this guide.)
- Knowing these historical facts also gives us more distance from the action.
- Perhaps tongue-in-cheek, Bolt lets the audience know that More's antagonists, except Rich, also suffered.

Interrogation

More's interrogation reveals the weakness of the charges and the apparent strength of maintaining silence as a defence, despite Cromwell's threat of torture, Norfolk's appeal to fellowship and Cranmer's attempt to find a saving compromise.

Cromwell is pressured for a result but knows Henry wouldn't allow More to be tortured. Perhaps he's struck by another possibility after hearing More insist that the law requires a fact: notice his response in the stage direction, '*looks at him and away again*' (p.77). The idea of manufacturing a 'fact' is possibly reinforced by hearing Cranmer's anxious warning to the Jailer not to commit perjury (for the huge reward Cromwell offers) if he's on oath to report something incriminating on More (p.80). Cromwell and Rich leave without having formulated the perjury but all the prerequisites are in place.

Q Why is the rack an important stage feature?

Q What does the Common Man mean when he says that the Jailer's job is 'nearer the knuckle than most' (p.75)?

Scene 15 (pp.81–8)

Summary: *More's family makes a short visit; Margaret can't persuade him to take the oath; the Jailer polices the visit, disclaiming responsibility as a 'simple man'.*

Under intense strain, Alice, Margaret and Roper struggle to have their last conversation with More. He teases them, then begins a recapitulation of key arguments about words, oaths and heroism.

Margaret provides More's last temptation to submit and deny his conscience. She tries several powerful openings:

- First she quotes More's own teaching: 'God more regards the thoughts of the heart than the words of the mouth' (p.83). More responds by stressing that an oath is about integrity to self.

- She argues that More elects to make himself a suffering hero. He expresses the complex relationship between virtues and sins in a beautifully structured speech (pp.83–4), reminiscent of the debate in *Utopia*. He can now justify heroism when it's a defining quality of staying human (p.84).
- She asks what God can reasonably want, which has been a preoccupation of More's. (Remember his outburst against God's subtlety, p.39.)
- She describes their home without him – this has the strongest effect. Like torture, it puts More on an emotional 'rack'.

Key point

More still insists: 'There'll be no trial, they have no case' (p.85). He does not yet know that Cromwell has 'evidence' to mount a trial. This is a good example of how theatre can take a well-known story or historical event and dramatise it in such a way that the audience goes with the process and can still be surprised.

More's impulse to share Alice's custard with Bishop Fisher (p.86) is an example of how his mischievously inappropriate wit betrays his fearful state of mind, anxious both for his own life and for his friend. Alice takes offence because the custard is her gift of love to him, and she is equally terrified of what will happen. The 'custard conversation' expresses their desperation to communicate at the deepest level for the last time.

Q Do you agree with Margaret's arguments? Do More's responses satisfy you?

Q Why does More tell his family to leave the country (p.85)?

Q How do you interpret More's cry against 'These plain, simple, men!' at the end of the scene (p.88)?

Scene 16 (pp.88–97)

Summary: *More's show trial and sentencing in Westminster Hall.*

The music, Cromwell's doggerel poetry about 'the Law' and the Common Man's elaborate stage setting announce that the scene is about theatre (as sensational trials frequently are). Bolt also draws on More's recorded speeches and writings to give the dialogue a theatrically heightened formality.

Before formally reading the charge, Cromwell opens his attack with 'news' about Bishop Fisher's execution (p.90). This is calculated to devastate More. Significantly, too, Cromwell's casually sadistic emphasis on 'the *late* Bishop Fisher' galvanises More into making his views publicly known through his final 'heroic' statements. (See Wilson 2001 for more details on Fisher.)

Cromwell's show trial has a foregone conclusion, although we don't know how it will develop yet. He sets out to demolish More's prime defence – his silence – by suggesting that it 'speaks' a particular meaning. We are in the difficult position of knowing that More's defence is a legal quibble masking the fact that he *does* deny the truth of the Act and the Oath.

Ideological positions are also on trial in this scene. More values an individual's integrity in terms of their commitment to their conscience and their soul, whereas Cromwell values loyalty to the state first (p.93). Rich says 'I do solemnly swear …' (p.93), but his oath on the Bible means nothing to him because he has decided to override his conscience – he's simply doing a favour to Cromwell in return for the gift of 'Wales'.

Q Why would the Common Man prefer not to be Foreman of the Jury?

Q See William Roper's 'The Life of Sir Thomas More' at www.fordham.edu/halsall/mod/16Croper-more.html for an account of what More said at his trial. What effect do you think More's actual words have on the dramatic impact of this scene in the play?

Q Research the Magna Carta and the Coronation Oath to understand how seriously More takes Cromwell's abuse of established legal procedure.

Scene 17 (pp.97–9)

Summary: *More's execution.*

More's beheading is not made into a big finale – historically, the King requested him to use few words. Notice how dramatic moments reinforce our idea of More, the modest man of conscience, facing death calmly:

- He refuses the drink from his friend Norfolk – who, in his official capacity, has just sentenced More. Note More's comparison with his 'master's' (Christ's) final drink – More seeks no comfort or relief at this point. This refusal is also More's farewell to Norfolk's 'fellowship'.
- He farewells Margaret calmly with words from his *Dialogue of Comfort* (written in 1534 in the Tower before books were taken away from him).
- He confronts the woman who tried to bribe him and comes to jeer – he still refuses to change his honest verdict.
- He refuses spiritual help from Cranmer, who represents outward piety but has no firm belief (hence his envy of More's calm).

Cromwell and Chapuys

The play concludes with Cromwell and Chapuys re-entering the stage following More's execution. Politically they are enemies – reflected by their initial *'postures of frozen hostility'* (p.99) – but ultimately they acknowledge that their similarities outweigh their differences. Each is an accomplished servant of the state that employs them; they have no real commitment to principles or beliefs other than self-preservation and personal advancement. As they leave the stage chuckling, it is left for the audience to reflect on what has been lost in the society in which such men thrive.

Q What do you think it means to be 'heroic' in the way More is shown to be?

Q Do you think it's appropriate that Cromwell exits with the props basket (p.98)?

Q Why is the Common Man made to play the executioner?

Alternative ending (p.101)

In the 1960 London production the play ended on a less cynical note, omitting the final meeting between Cromwell and Chapuys and concluding with the Common Man addressing the audience. This generates a stronger sense of closure – and perhaps of reassurance – since the Common Man also begins the play with a direct address to the audience. Though less sinister in its tone, this ending asks audience members to relate the play's events to their own lives and values, so is equally provocative in its own way.

Q How does this ending alter the way an audience would focus on what has happened to More?

Q Which ending do you prefer as theatre?

CHARACTERS & RELATIONSHIPS

Bolt's characters all have strong individual qualities but are at the same time representative of points of view or approaches to living 'politically' in Henry VIII's court – More is said to have called it 'having fun with tamed lions ... suddenly the fun becomes fatal'.

We engage with dramatic characters in 'realist' mode because they sound and behave as people like us – we notice More's barely suppressed fear at moments in his interrogations, Norfolk's quick temper, Cromwell's irritation with the treacherous crawler Rich, Alice's rough and deep affection for the husband she simply can't understand. We also notice that these characters play roles in an emerging debate about political, philosophical and spiritual ideas: we soon understand why there are bound to be inevitable conflicts with dangerous consequences, when 'the fun becomes fatal'.

The Common Man

Key quotes

'Is this a costume? ... A bit of black material to reduce Old Adam to the Common Man.' (p.1)

'The Sixteenth Century is the Century of the Common Man ... Like all the other centuries.' (p.2)

'The great thing's not to get out of your depth ...' (p.24)

An 'Everyman' figure

The Common Man represents 'that which is common to us all', an 'Everyman' figure. He is an eternal performer of roles: he aims to survive, pass the buck, and live an untroubled life. He also has an important dual function in the play, relating (without close personal involvement) to the other characters and also relating to the audience as Chorus, commentator and goad to conscience.

He is an ordinary man but not meant to be seen as vulgar (crude and off-putting). Bolt 'meant him to be attractive, and his philosophy impregnable' – he's meant to make us laugh, but with a 'rueful note of recognition' (pp.xviii–xix). The key word here is 'rueful' – why?

Note how he responds to different characters, adapting himself to suit the occasion. He is 'contemptuous' of Rich (p.2) but will become his steward (pp.61–2) out of self-interest – a 'servant who can handle the boss' type. Only More really challenges his chosen existential status. More's 'Bless you' to Matthew is genuine – and a reminder to take the idea of blessing seriously (p.2) – as is More's sincere 'I shall miss you, Matthew' (p.57). Matthew reacts angrily because More's affection challenges his wish for an uncommitted role: 'don't you complicate the job by putting things in me for me to miss!' (p.57).

The Common Man as actor

The Common Man opens the play as an 'actor' – someone who deserves a proper costume. He assumes the role and name of Matthew, household steward first to More, then to Rich. Lacking any genuine spirituality and wishing for none, he's ironically but appropriately named: in Christian iconography the four evangelists are symbolised by lion (Mark), eagle (John), bull (Luke) and man (Matthew).

His actor's complaint about an inadequate costume is important because it draws attention to how costumes will define his function in the play. Various costume changes will denote his performance of roles that exonerate him from responsibility for events – he is just doing his job, obeying orders, making no personal investment. Nevertheless, as the play's events make clear, he is fundamentally involved in actions of real political, legal and moral significance.

Sir Thomas More

Key quotes

'The service of God is not a dishonour to any office.' (p.26)

'I neither could nor would rule my King ... But there's a little ... little, area ... where I must rule myself.' (p.35)

'... perhaps we *must* stand fast a little – even at the risk of being heroes.' (to Margaret, p.84)

'The man's utterly unreliable!' (Chapuys, p.64)

'It takes a lot of education to get a man as deep as that ... And a deep nature to begin with too.' (The Common Man, p.41)

There is a great deal of dramatic tension in More's character because he is genuinely religious but aware of the lure of martyrdom for his kind of personality (p.2). Chapuys reinforces this idea by reminding More he's called 'the English Socrates' by his friend Erasmus (p.49). The audience can understand his fear as well as his determination to stay true to his conscience – especially when Cromwell accuses him of putting up a 'noble motive' for what is really 'frivolous self-conceit' (p.92).

Key point

More wants to survive, but not at the cost of his soul.

More doesn't want conventional political power; he is 'commanded into office' (p.5). Compare his ideas with Wolsey's, Norfolk's and Cromwell's, and notice how he uses flattery 'with just a soupcon of discreet impudence' (p.35) to be diplomatic to Henry.

Because of his demonstrably high moral 'status', other characters look to him to provide what they lack or need. This is a dangerous situation because he can't satisfy their needs without compromising himself. So:

- Henry says he wants an honest man as his conscience but needs More to agree to his divorce; results in Henry's accusation that he is a 'traitorous' subject (p.69).
- Both Wolsey and Cromwell want More's spiritual backing for controversial state decisions, especially those with ramifications in Europe.
- Rich needs the patronage of a 'good man' to offset his Machiavellian inclinations.
- Roper has visions of the widely admired More as a martyr for religious reform.

- Norfolk wants an easy fellowship uncomplicated by principles or introspection.
- Chapuys wants an influential European moral 'voice' to back Queen Catherine's cause.
- Alice wants a safe husband who'll relish his high social status.
- Margaret wants her beloved philosopher father to stay alive, to 'say the words … and in your heart think otherwise' (p.83).

See the further discussion of More in terms of his relationships with other central characters under Norfolk and More and Cromwell and More below.

Thomas Howard, Duke of Norfolk

Key quotes

> '*We're* supposed to be the arrogant ones, the proud, splenetic ones – and we've all given in!' (p.71)
>
> 'I'm not a scholar ... and frankly I don't know whether the marriage was lawful or not ... Can't you do what I did, and come with us, for fellowship?' (p.78)

The Duke of Norfolk was also Earl Marshall of England, the state's chief law-enforcer. He displays a conventional sense of loyalty to the Crown, pride, status and proper form, as in his criticism of More for insulting 'the King and His Council in the person of the Lord Archbishop (p.77). He is politically and intellectually slower than More, though far from stupid, and participates in interrogations without properly understanding the details of More's position.

Norfolk's bluff crudity, evident in the opening scene, typifies an 'aristocratic' personality: he finds Alice's roughness easier to share than More's subtleties. He has an undeveloped religious belief, and gives no moral opinion on Henry's divorce. (Interestingly, the historical Norfolk was uncle to two of Henry's wives – Anne Boleyn and Catherine Howard – and supervised both their executions.)

Norfolk and More

Key quotes

'I'm fond of you, and there it is! You're fond of me, and there it is!' (Norfolk, p.71)

'... we've had a quarrel since the day we met, our friendship was but sloth.' (More, p.72)

There is a strong affection between Norfolk and More, though it is severely tested by the play's events. Their contrasting personalities make the friendship interesting to both men: compare Norfolk's casual blasphemies ('Well, damn my soul') to More's real respect for soul; or the way Norfolk recognises and can absorb More's greater capacity for cruel comments (p.72). More's quarrelsome point about pedigree (p.73) appears to fracture the bond between them.

Norfolk is slightly shamed by More's steadfastness, which he dimly comprehends – but he nonetheless sentences his friend to death (pp.96–7).

- Central scenes for this relationship are Scene 9 (pp.51–4) and Scene 13 (pp.70–3).

Thomas Cromwell

Key quotes

'A *farrier's* son? ... It'll be up quick and down quick with Master Cromwell.' (Alice, p.7)

'When the King wants something done, I do it.' (p.21)

Cromwell's prime aim (as the play depicts him) is to survive and advance his career by getting things done for the King (p.21). As such, cynical pragmatism is the key to his character – as is evident, for instance, when he praises Rich for admitting he has a price (p.43), or offers the Jailer a bribe of fifty guineas to get 'evidence' against More (p.80). His only match as a political strategist is the Common Man playing the Publican of 'The Loyal Subject', saying 'I don't understand, sir' (p.41).

Cromwell can be sadistic (he burns Rich's hand, p.46) and, as More puts it, 'threaten like a dockside bully' (p.79); he is also a devious but effective 'Minister of State', claiming to serve 'the King' and his 'great native country!' (p.93).

Cromwell and More

Historically, Cromwell and More knew each other: Cromwell visited More and admired him. Their different views of the individual's role in the state divided them ideologically. However, Bolt makes the moral distinction between them simpler in the play than it was in reality.

Cromwell's idea of a loyal subject is someone who makes no trouble, obeys instructions and feels slightly anxious about having ideas. In this view, private thoughts of individuals need to be policed because they may be seditious, or simply contain information that can be used for Cromwell's advantage.

In contrast, More represents the antithesis of Cromwell's compliant model citizen. More's religious practice gives him a moral focus beyond the state, he values privacy of thought and feeling, he resists bullying, and he values and stands by dictates of conscience.

These two characters are diametrically opposed intelligent people, who recognise each other's qualities. More says Cromwell is 'a very able man ... Yes, I say he is' (irritated by Rich, p.3) and Cromwell says of More: '*there's* an innocent man ... Yes, I say he is' (irritated by Rich, p.44).

Cromwell and Signor Chapuys (the Spanish Ambassador)

Key quotes

'Goodness presents its own difficulties.' (Chapuys, p.62)

'(*Admiring*) Oho – beware these professional diplomats.' (Cromwell, p.21)

Examine these like-minded ruthless state servants who track each other through the play and would agree on 'goodness' presenting 'difficulties'. They are enemies, yet they are remarkably similar in their beliefs and political practices. See Scenes 3 (pp.14–15), 5 (pp.21–4) and the play's conclusion (p.99) for exchanges between Cromwell and Chapuys. Their activities manipulate and entrap others – except the Common Man as the Steward, who has their measure (pp.22–4).

King Henry

Key quotes

'What else but a fool to live in a Court, in a licentious mob – when I have friends, with gardens.' (p.30)

'If you could come with me, you are the man I would soonest raise – yes, with my own hand.' (to More, p.34)

'All the world knows Your Grace's book, asserting the seven sacraments of the Church.' (Margaret to Henry, p.29)

'Then know that the King commands me … to tell you that there never was nor never could be so villainous a servant nor so traitorous a subject as yourself!' (Cromwell to More, p.69)

Henry's unstable egocentric personality is often displayed – his mood switches back and forth from affability to irritable brooding to aggressiveness. He claims to want More's opinion but at the same time doesn't listen, is rude and overbearing in conversation and intolerant of criticism.

He believes his soul is in peril because his marriage is against divine law, but since he argued in defence of sacraments in his 1521 book, his conscience is conflicted now that he wants a divorce. While he accepts Margaret's flattery of his scholarship, he hints at More's involvement in writing – now that its contents are an embarrassment. Cromwell later uses this authorship question to accuse More of leading the King's thoughts astray.

Another side to Henry's character is reflected in the way he advertises himself as a Renaissance prince – scholar, musician, navigator – then fantasises about the quiet life in More's garden (p.30).

More's honest support is essential to square Henry's conscience. Henry encapsulates his need for such support in talking about his followers, identifying Cromwell accurately as one of the 'jackals with sharp teeth' (p.32).

Cardinal Wolsey

Key quotes

'More! You should have been a cleric!' ... 'Like yourself, Your Grace?' (Wolsey and More, p.13)

'If Wolsey fell, the splash would swamp a few small boats like ours.' (More, pp.19–20)

Wolsey is the most powerful man in England after the King. He controls state and Church business until the divorce issue causes Henry to turn against him. More's 'boat' is 'swamped' indirectly by Wolsey's fall – he becomes Chancellor on Wolsey's recommendation and is faced with the same insoluble royal issue.

Wolsey needs More's help to lobby the Pope for a declaration that Henry's marriage to Catherine was invalid. However, he resents More who can't 'see facts flat on, without that moral squint' (p.10), because this complicates his own 'down to earth' grasp of political realities – and highlights his moral shortcomings as a cleric.

Richard Rich

Key quotes

'Sir Thomas, if only you knew how much, much rather I'd [be] yours than his!' (to More about Cromwell, p.7)

'Father, that man's bad.' (Margaret, p.38)

'I'm only anxious to do what is correct, Secretary.' (to Cromwell, p.61)

Resist any impulse to feel sorry for Rich. In Bolt's characterisation he is not someone who would have turned out differently had More supported him better (i.e. in accordance with his vanity and ambition rather than by recommending a good but modest post with the Dean of St Paul's). Rich is characterised as a self-serving betrayer, craving support for moral weakness but profiting by supposed 'lost innocence' (p.44). He evolves into a classic 'public servant' toady under Cromwell's tutelage and his cool act of perjury condemns More to death.

Note how these incidents shed light on Rich's scheming personality:

- Rich tells More's family he's attracted by Cromwell's methods (p.3) and likes him (p.7); he tries to quote Cromwell's ideas on Machiavelli but is cut off by Norfolk (p.7).
- He resists More's advice to 'go where he won't be tempted' (p.4).
- He takes the bribe cup eagerly from More – ashamed of his need rather than the fact it's associated with an attempted bribe, he'll sell it for 'decent clothes' (p.4). Later he embarrasses Cromwell, who attempts to frame More for bribery with the cup, by forgetting that Norfolk was present when he was given it (p.61).
- In his trial, More gives a contemptuous summing-up of Rich's character; repetition serves to convey how deeply offended More is by Rich's barefaced lie on oath: 'Is it probable – is it probable – that after so long a silence, on this, the very point so urgently sought of me, I should open my mind *to such a man as that?*' (p.94; my emphasis).

Alice More

Key quotes

'I know I'm a fool. But I'm no such fool as at this time to be lamenting for my dresses! Or to relish complimenting on my custard!' (p.85)

'I'll tell you what I'm afraid of; that when you've gone, I shall hate you for it.' (p.86)

Despite her snobbish protestation that she's a knight's wife who can ride with lords, Alice is an archetypal 'city wife' in her character – bossy, argumentative, stubbornly illiterate, not intimidated by Norfolk (pp.5–7) nor afraid to give her 'opinion of the King and his Council' (p.86). She is nonetheless an obedient wife who lives with a bitter sense that More loves his clever daughter better than her. Alice's love and respect for More is expressed intensely at their last meeting (pp.85–6), although she admits she doesn't 'believe this had to happen' (p.86).

Note Alice's protectiveness towards More in her honest outspokenness. She knows Wolsey wants to discuss 'the Queen's business' with More rather than 'the King's business' when he's summoned in the middle of the night (p.8). She warns Roper, 'You'd dance him to the block! ... Scattering hymn-books in his path!' and warns More with the obvious truth that he won't simply be left 'to learn to fish' (p.55). Alice lacks deep understanding of what More is trying to do but her loving impulses are good and steadfast.

More needs Alice's rough common sense to keep him grounded in reality (e.g. reminding him of the danger of catching a 'cold in the head', p.19). She fears that he doesn't care for her safety, though, as her 'too fat to hide' comment suggests (p.40).

Margaret More

Key quotes

'Amazing girl, Thomas, but where are you going to find a husband for her?' (Norfolk, p.7)

'Oh – why you don't beat that girl!' ... 'No, no, she's full of education – and it's a delicate commodity.' (Alice and More, pp.18–19)

'Oh, you'd walk on the bottom of the sea and think yourself a crab if he suggested it!' (Alice, p.55)

'You have long known the secrets of my heart.' (More to Margaret, p.98)

Characterised as an intelligent and loving daughter, Margaret is her father's smart adversary and confidante at home. She waits up for him (p.9) – if he doesn't tell her something, it's a sign he's worried (as the Common Man tells Cromwell, p.23).

- Her gentleness is stressed throughout, e.g. she is shocked by Norfolk's hunting hawk, asking 'Did he kill the heron?' (p.6); More provides a reassuring answer for her – 'the heron got home to his chicks' (p.6); she stops Henry bullying Norfolk (p.28).
- Her witty humour is like More's; she shocks Norfolk with her teasing approval of Machiavelli's book: 'Very practical, Your Grace' (p.7).
- Her early suspicion of Rich shows her sharp judgement of character: 'Do you *like* Master Cromwell, Master Rich?' (p.7).

William Roper

Key quotes

'Nice boy ... Terribly strong principles, though.' (More, p.18)

'Must everything be made convenient? I'm not a convenient man, Meg – I've got an inconvenient conscience!' (p.36)

'... this was not practical; (*resonant*) this was moral!' (to More, p.55)

'While we are witty, the Devil may enter us unawares.' (p.66)

Roper is passionate, with strong but changeable religious views. He is persistent in love, despite More's initial objection, and is allowed to marry Margaret; their warm relationship is evident throughout. Roper's loyalty to More is demonstrated by his behaviour during the family's prison visit (pp.81–7).

- Roper's arguments with More about the law and oaths help to clarify ideas for the audience.
- The historical William Roper wrote 'The Life of Sir Thomas More' (see www.fordham.edu/halsall/mod/16Croper-more.html), one of Bolt's sources.

Chapuys

Key quotes

'Sir Thomas, I will be plain with you ... plain, that is, so far as the diplomatic decencies permit.' (p.15)

Chapuys is a repulsively 'diplomatic' ambassador who expresses traditional Catholic piety (hence the Common Man's ironic 'very religious man', p.24). Despite warning that 'No man can serve two masters, Steward' (p.24), he demonstrates that he puts service to the King of Spain's interests before religious principles. He thus plays the same game as Cromwell but on the opposite political 'team' – they understand each other very well, as is shown by their joint exit at the play's end.

Chapuys also sharpens More's thinking about his own motives in two ways:

- He plays the role of tempter to More, suggesting saintliness and martyrdom; Chapuys knows that More's death would serve the old Church's cause in Europe.
- He clarifies More's dilemma as a statesman with religious belief, who can be inactive only up to a point, after which 'one is not merely "compromised", one is in truth corrupted' (p.50).

Thomas Cranmer

Key quotes

'But that you owe obedience to your King is not capable of question. So weigh a doubt against a certainty – and sign.' (to More, pp.78–9)

'You're very sure of that, Sir Thomas.'
(to More, who anticipates being sent to God, p.99)

As Archbishop of Canterbury, Cranmer is the spiritual leader of the new 'Church of England' Catholics, and is instrumental in making the Church 'a wing of the Palace' (Roper's accurate view, p.48). Unlike More, he is prepared to adjust his spiritual allegiance to conform to political realities for the good of the state. His conscience (perhaps) makes him very sensitive whenever he's onstage with More.

Q Research Thomas Cranmer, who (like More) showed real courage and found a place in history by his death. He was burned alive as a heretic in the reign of Mary I, daughter of Henry and Catherine of Aragon.

A woman (Catherine Anger)

Key quotes

'When you were Chancellor, you gave a false judgement against me. Remember that now.' (p.98)

The woman from Lincoln who sent More a silver cup worth a hundred shillings hears Cromwell tell Norfolk that More did accept her bribe (p.59). She is then dismissed before hearing that More gave the cup away to Rich. Cromwell agrees with More's judgement against her. Nevertheless, she reappears at More's execution to jeer because she thinks he's cheated her – since she paid her bribe and expected his legal cooperation.

Her minor presence in the play illustrates again how More's ethical standards run contrary to the way of the world. The damage her small corruption is capable of facilitating runs from beginning to end.

Chapuys's attendant

Key quotes

'I wish your mother had chosen some other career for you; you've no political sense whatever.' (Chapuys, p.63)

Chapuys's young attendant makes an interesting comparison with Rich as a trainee servant of state. He lacks Rich's instincts as a junior 'jackal' to know which side to favour – hence Chapuys's sharp comments. Does he learn anything about diplomacy from a model like Chapuys?

THEMES, IDEAS & VALUES

A careful study of *A Man for All Seasons* makes us realise that there are no simple or universal answers to questions about individual conscience. Like people today, Bolt's historical characters have grown up with their own values concerning life and duty, so they behave in different ways when challenged. How we respond to them in the play's fictional world can help us to think more carefully about what values we hold, and how we might respond to similarly confronting situations.

I have identified four main thematic 'clusters':

- the individual and the state
- law and the individual
- religion and the individual
- the individual in society.

Each of these themes is broken down into a number of subsections. These direct you to moments in the text that explore different aspects of the overall theme by illustrating specific ideas and values held by characters.

The individual and the state

People in modern societies generally expect (and agree) to have their lives controlled through laws made by the state (i.e. the central government of the country), in return for efficient daily functioning and social stability. To what extent the individual will (or ought to) tolerate supervision in matters of belief or freedom of expression is a significant ongoing debate. Most people conform (at least outwardly) despite some disagreements with the state's actions or statements; Cromwell claims that an appearance of conformity is 'all we need' (p.58).

In Tudor England the general population experienced a period of relative social stability maintained by tight controls, especially regarding individual liberties to speak and act. Unorthodox religious views and criticism of the monarch were rigorously policed. Public execution – by being hanged, drawn and quartered for treason – was intended to be a graphically horrible deterrent to others. Remember that, until the King grants him the mercy of beheading, Thomas More expects to face a traitor's public death, hence his fear expressed to Alice about 'the worst that they may do to me' (p.85, and see note, p.117).

The play explores this theme in several ways. The argument rests on two well-worn political clichés that define the moral issues for every character: 'Every man has his price' (derived from Machiavelli) and 'No man can serve two masters' (Matthew 6:24).

State demands and private conscience

Key quotes

'I believe, when statesmen forsake their own private conscience for the sake of their public duties ... they lead their country by a short route to chaos.' (More to Wolsey, p.12)

'Your conscience is your own affair; but you are my Chancellor!' (King to More, p.33)

'The King's a man of conscience and he wants either Sir Thomas More to bless his marriage or Sir Thomas More destroyed.' (Cromwell, p.70)

'In matters of conscience, the loyal subject is more bounden to be loyal to his conscience than to any other thing.' (More to Cromwell, p.92)

Wolsey's interview with More picks up a key point about the state servant's loyalties. More's dilemma is that he wants to be the King's good servant but thinks a servant's duty is to advise honestly, not pander to the royal will or the pretence that Henry has a 'conscience' that is anything but self-serving. He is even more direct in his criticism of Cromwell's unethical methods (pp.92–6).

Because they are based on his spiritual values, More's views express a serious ethical challenge to Cardinal Wolsey's manipulation of worldly power and Cromwell's expedient approach to carrying out royal orders. Neither way, in More's view, serves the state properly.

Public duty and private friendship

Key quotes

'I'll tell the King of your loyalty to your friend.' (Cromwell to Norfolk, p.60)

A duty is an act that carries a very strong moral or legal obligation. Your sense of duty is closely related to your values and what you think is right or wrong in your conscience. It may be, though, that at times there will be a conflict between different types of duty.

What duty does an individual owe to the state and to other individuals (such as friends and family)? Should all public duties be carried out without question? Duty is often associated with loyalty: both can be tested in a crisis. The perceived demands of duty may put pressure on personal bonds like friendship and family ties – or be used as a lever to divide loyalties (Norfolk) or induce betrayal (Rich).

Consider how the play investigates the following aspects of duty and friendship:

- a public servant's duty (Wolsey, More, Cromwell, Rich)
- a priest's duty (Cardinal Wolsey, Archbishop Cranmer)
- a monarch's duty to kingdom (Henry)
- a family's duty to its members (More, Alice, Margaret, Roper, Matthew)
- a friend's duty (Norfolk, More).

'Friend' is a charged word in the play: notice how Rich, Cromwell and Henry use it to manipulate situations. Cromwell frightens Norfolk, 'known to have been a friend of More's', before explaining that his 'participation' is necessary to give the appearance of legal fair play in More's arrest (p.60). Cromwell pressures Norfolk to choose between supporting his friend and demonstrating loyalty to the King. At More's trial, Norfolk does his duty as Earl Marshall of England and reads the death sentence to his friend (p.97). More is a friend to Norfolk when he gives honest warning of 'the times' and later stages a quarrel to sever ties for Norfolk's own safety (pp.72–3).

Realpolitik

Key quotes

'You lay traps for me!' ... 'No, I show you the times.' (Norfolk and More, p.53)

'[More's] wilful indifference to realities which were obvious to quite ordinary contemporaries ...' (the Common Man quoting a 'historian', p.20)

This term (from nineteenth-century German politics) describes political policy-making based on power and expediency rather than ideals. It joins self-interest to the use of power to do what the state says needs to be done even though it may not be quite as moral as you'd like.

In the working out of Tudor 'realpolitik' surrounding Henry's divorce, Bolt's characters experience either a collision or intersection between personal morality and 'the times'. Rich is the antithesis of More and a perfect example of a man who adjusts himself to the times, if and when the price is right.

The play emphasises the moral distinction between two able people: More has an understanding of the world he lives in but no desire to be opportunistic, whereas Cromwell is untroubled by conscience and driven by self-interest. More understands the danger (as he sees it) of giving Cromwell unlimited power (p.13), and Cromwell certainly uses unconstitutional manipulation to 'do things' (p.21) that the King wants done.

Cromwell argues the danger of More's moral fixity in his critique of men who are '"upright", "steadfast", men who want themselves to be the constant factor in the situation. Which of course they can't be' (p.45). He's aware that the unstoppable historical 'situation rolls forward in any case' (p.45): a political realist either goes with it or gets out of the way.

Recognition and status

Key quotes

'Why not be a teacher?' ... 'And if I was who would know it?' (More and Rich, p.4)

'Yes, it may be that I am a little intoxicated ... with success! And who has a strong head for success? None of us gets enough of it.' (Cromwell, p.42)

'In any state that was half good, you would be raised up high, not here, for what you've done already.' (Margaret to More, p.83)

As Henry's Chancellor, Cardinal Wolsey carved out for himself tremendous power, wealth and status. Cromwell usually shows less interest in outward displays of success but, like Wolsey, wields power to retain his controlling status with the King.

Rich epitomises the young career opportunist for whom teaching is too humble a profession: track his rise through public office as the play develops. In a key scene with Cromwell, Rich articulates his version of the Machiavellian dictum that 'every man has his price', when he says that 'It would depend what I was offered' (p.43).

In contrast, More has a high status – he is internationally known for his ideas, and people want his support and value his honesty – but is very reluctant to accept the material advantages of public office. He rejects the woman's bribe, and prefers not to wear the Chancellor's gold chain for Henry. Norfolk makes a plain assessment of More's modest wealth – 'When was there last a Chancellor whose possessions after three years in office totalled one hundred pounds and a gold chain' (p.58) – as a testament to his exemplary ethical standards.

Convenience

Key quotes

'Must everything be made convenient? ... I've got an inconvenient conscience!' (Roper, p.36)

'Sophistication ... The Court has corrupted you ... you have learnt to study your "convenience"; you have learnt to flatter!' (Roper to More, p.36)

The two scenes at the end of Act One raise the key idea of 'convenience', which has a different meaning for different characters:

- Roper rejects convenience, asserting that he is 'not a convenient man' (p.36); he insists on his moral right to denounce More's caution when he thinks fit, though Margaret warns him politely that his timing is 'not convenient' (p.35) – just after Henry's exit, when everyone's nervous and uncomfortable. More as Lord Chancellor could have him punished for slander or worse.
- Cromwell, on the other hand, endorses the idea of convenience; he describes how administration looks for the key 'constant factor' before permitting or preventing individual actions according to whether or not they are 'convenient' for the state.

Law and the individual

Key quotes

> 'But then why these Justices, Chancellors, Admirals?' ... 'Oh, *they* are the constitution. Our ancient, English constitution. I merely do things.' (Chapuys and Cromwell, p.21)
>
> 'I'd give the Devil benefit of law, for my own safety's sake.' (More, p.39)
>
> 'The law is a causeway upon which so long as he keeps to it a citizen may walk safely.' (More, p.92)

The English legal system is still considered to rest on – and honour – precepts of Common Law, which has evolved over centuries and been agreed to (not always willingly) by monarchs and parliaments. The Common Law is set down in documents like the Magna Carta to protect people's rights and be a 'shelter' against unjust persecution.

The core of this theme is expressed in Bolt's opening remarks:

> the Law ... is the very pattern of society. More's trust in the law was his trust in his society; his desperate sheltering beneath the forms of the law was his determination to remain within the shelter of society. (Preface, p.xv)

In fact, though, as Cromwell cynically demonstrates, it isn't difficult to subvert legal process by enacting new laws or committing perjury, especially when there is no separation of powers between government and judiciary. The play illustrates 'Cromwell's contemptuous shattering of the forms of law' (Preface, p.xv), utilising Rich's blatant perjury – against which More, or anyone else, is defenceless.

Follow More's extended imagery of the law as either dry land (a causeway) or a sheltering forest, with himself as forester hiding among trees and in thickets (p.39). Contrast this with his imagery of sailing or being on the sea, which always signifies danger. Note his criticism of Roper's dangerous 'seagoing principles' (p.39). Also, contrast Cromwell's ominous rhetoric of his 'good, plain sailor's art' to 'fix these quicksands' (i.e. More's evasive wits, p.89).

The letter of the law as a defence

Key quotes

'... it must be done by law. It's just a matter of finding the right law. Or making one.' (Cromwell, p.61)

'The law requires more than an assumption; the law requires a fact.' (More, p.77)

More's reliance on the letter of the law rather than assumptions or inferences about 'meaning' is a clever but dangerous ploy. Ironically, what brings More down in the end is not an application of the law (old or new), but a false 'fact' – Rich's perjury (p.94), devised by Cromwell.

What's legal or what's right?

Key quotes

'I know what's legal not what's right. And I'll stick to what's legal.' (More, p.38)

'The currents and eddies of right and wrong, which you find such plain-sailing, I can't navigate, I'm no voyager.' (More to Roper, p.39)

Is the law absolute, enshrined in statutes – or flexible, open to change to suit particular cases and historical times? This is still a key issue today, when legislation enacted to deal with perceived threats may challenge established statutes and weaken safeguards against excessive state control over individual freedoms.

More's comment about navigating 'right and wrong' raises important philosophical and ethical points. The law itself and sentencing are not about imposing subjective moral judgements but about being accurate with evidence. Compare this with Cromwell's idea of administrative 'convenience' (i.e. who wants what outcome?) – for Cromwell, the 'right' thing to do bears little relation to what is legal or what the 'facts' are, since these can always be changed or manipulated to suit the present political purpose.

Keeping silent or speaking out

Key quotes

'Look, what I know I'll say!' (Roper, p.17)

'... in silence is my safety under the law, but my silence must be absolute ...' (More, p.56)

'This "silence" of his is bellowing up and down Europe!' (Cromwell, pp.57–8)

In response to Cromwell's speech about 'many kinds of silence' (p.91), More quibbles to protect himself by quoting the legal maxim that silence indicates consent: *qui tacet consentire* (p.92). But can a dissenting conscience protect itself through silence? Can a person's views be inferred from their silence?

Roper's rash outspokenness about Court politics and religion could lead to his arrest for sedition or High Treason (p.48). He's protected (as Meg's partner) by More's calm intelligence in not exercising his authority as Chancellor. Note More's speech to Margaret and Roper about serving God 'wittily, in the tangle of [our] mind' and trying not to cause trouble: 'Our natural business lies in escaping' injustice – only when 'there is no escaping ... then we may clamour like champions' (p.74).

Religion and the individual

This theme again explores several related lines of thought:

- A strongly held religious belief guides a person's life, shaping values and ethical responses to things that happen in the world.
- Religious ideas may be sanctioned or tolerated by the state, or be independently held – sometimes with dangerous consequences for individuals or groups.
- How religion is practised in the state, what's demanded in its name, may strain individual conscience and challenge values. Archbishop Cranmer serves the King first ('convenience' again), whereas More upholds his own belief and conscience.

Church and state

Key quotes

'The Church is already a wing of the Palace is it not?' (Roper, p.48)

'You and your class have "given in" … because the religion of this country means nothing to you one way or the other.' (More to Norfolk, p.72)

In Tudor England, people's spiritual obedience to the Pope in Rome was literally re-formed, with Henry VIII proclaimed by Act of Parliament in 1531 as 'protector and only Supreme Head of the Church and Clergy in England'. Many people of conscience, including clergy, suffered the consequences of openly objecting to the change.

Henry's theological book *A Defence of the Seven Sacraments* (1521), written to refute Luther's heretical arguments, is the subject of key conversations with Henry (p.29) and Cromwell (pp.68–9). More appreciates the bitter irony of the present crisis over the royal divorce, in that Henry's book had been a defence of papal authority – which earned him the title 'Defender of the Faith' from Rome (p.68).

Reformation issues underpin every important conversation, such as the dialogue between Roper and More about the Convocation of bishops and the additional wording in the Act of Supremacy: 'so far as the law of

God allows', designed to be a defensive legal quibble about something that can't be known (p.48). More resigns the Chancellorship when Norfolk brings news that 'we've severed the connection with Rome' (p.52).

More's remarks to Norfolk about the English nobility's lack of concern for religion is meant seriously: they are unlikely to criticise Henry's behaviour or defend religious values. Norfolk makes several half-hearted attempts but is too easily put down by Cromwell. Cardinal Wolsey is example of a worldly priest who manipulates Vatican politics to serve his own (and the state's) interests, and he openly sneers at More's belief in prayer as a basis for governing the country (p.11).

Genuine spirituality or conventional show of piety?

Key quotes

'You must consider, Thomas, that I stand in peril of my soul.' (Henry, p.31)

'Are you sure you're not religious?' ... 'Almost sure' ... 'Get sure.' (Cromwell and Rich, p.43)

In Bolt's play, Henry's Christian views (such as his concern for his soul and anger at the 'Bishop of Rome') are related almost entirely to his position of power; they are manipulated to serve his royal will. More believes that Henry retains a trace of Christian values in that he won't perjure himself (p.69). Cromwell (a cannier psychologist than More?) knows that his job is to assuage Henry's guilty 'conscience' by focusing blame elsewhere. As he says to Rich, 'we've made ourselves the keepers of this conscience. And it's ravenous' (p.70).

More's Catholicism is the antithesis of Henry's; it involves a daily ritual carried out in humility and domestic privacy. His crude retort to Chapuys's fake piety – 'To make contact with a brother in Christ you have only to open your window and empty a chamberpot' (p.49) – is meant to make the audience laugh. He mocks Roper at times, too, but treats him more respectfully overall because Roper has genuine principles.

Religious and political crisis: Henry's divorce

Key quotes

'I have no Queen! Catherine is not my wife and no priest can make her so, and they that say she is my wife are not only liars ... but Traitors! Mind it, Thomas!' (pp.33–4)

'A dispensation was given so that the King might marry Queen Catherine, for state reasons. Now are we to ask the Pope to – dispense with his dispensation, also for state reasons?' (More to Wolsey, pp.11–12)

The first warning to More that he could be charged as a traitor occurs with Henry's frustrated outburst at his polite resistance (pp.33–4), follows through to Cromwell's charging him 'with great ingratitude' in the King's name (p.69) and culminates in the formal charge of treason for offending the King (p.89). Cromwell spells out the need to project guilt onto More as 'a bad man, the kind of man a man of conscience *ought* to destroy' (p.70).

Alice accuses More of offending the King by standing between Henry and Anne Boleyn. He corrects her by asserting that 'what stands between them is a sacrament of the Church' (p.35). Later, More repeats his view that Henry's 'war on the Pope' is 'because the Pope will not declare that our Queen is not his wife' (p.52).

The individual in society

Key quotes

'You'll forfeit all you've got – which includes the respect of your country – for a theory?' (Norfolk to More, p.53)

'What you have hunted me for is not my actions, but the thoughts of my heart. It is a long road you have opened. For first men will disclaim their hearts and presently they will have no hearts.' (More, p.95)

Two elements are significant to a mature 'self' as Bolt depicts More: integrity and conscience, both of which are expressed when a person is asked to take an oath.

Integrity is the quality of being honest with oneself and acting in a way that is consistent with one's core beliefs and values. For instance, More insists that by resigning as Chancellor he is not just making a 'noble gesture' for everyone to see and admire (which would flatter his ego) but is acting with integrity – in accordance with his deepest beliefs and principles.

Conscience (the interior monitor of right and wrong) may be a shaping moral force in individual behaviour, or it can be suppressed. Henry cannot tolerate living with his 'bad conscience'. More defends his deep belief, his religious 'theory', against Norfolk's criticism because it is his core 'self' – it's a matter of conscience; he must defend what he believes is right.

More's sad comment on 'hearts' pinpoints what he considers to be the destructive nature of Cromwell's conscience-free pragmatism: people who give up believing ('disclaim') what they know in their hearts will ultimately cease to care about moral issues at all and do nothing to prevent abuses of power. As a warning sign of social breakdown, it is still an issue that is debated strongly.

Bolt's 'hero of selfhood'

Key quotes

'... what matters to me is not whether it's true or not but that I believe it to be true, or rather not that I *believe* it, but that *I* believe it ...' (More, p.53)

'Is there no single sinew in the midst of this that serves no appetite of Norfolk's but is, just, Norfolk?' (More, p.73)

'What's *in* me for *him* to miss ...?' (the Common Man, p.57)

More challenges Norfolk to look into his core being, beyond just 'being a lord'. Like most people, Norfolk is unused to rigorous introspection and is uncomfortable with it. Similarly, the Common Man actively resents being prompted by More to recognise his lasting effect on someone else because it threatens to complicate his habitual lack of involvement with people and events.

More identifies his soul with his self in a key dialogue with Cromwell, after being accused of 'self-conceit'. More's ethical values are based in Christian belief so he naturally equates the impulses of his deepest inner being (his self, the 'I') with the most sacred element within him: 'a man's soul is his self!' (p.93).

Interestingly, the Common Man resents More's personal farewell because it threatens to turn him into a personality with a 'self' as opposed to a series of 'roles'. If he were a character he'd have to become more involved and committed; instead, he uses his performance of roles as a way of disavowing responsibility for his actions.

Oaths

Key quotes

'When a man takes an oath, Meg, he's holding his own self in his own hands. Like water …' (More, p.83)

'Now I will take an oath! If what Master Rich has said is true, then I pray I may never see God in the face! Which I would not say were it otherwise for anything on earth.' (More, p.94)

The scenes in which More has his last meeting with his family and is then tried for treason draw together key ideas about oath-taking for More as a sacred commitment. For him, nothing can have greater value than being true to one's word, taking care to understand words, and valuing words as expressions of integrity. Hence, for More, the significance of keeping silent or refusing to endorse some words.

More says: 'What is an oath then but words we say to God?' (p.83). However, Margaret has sworn an oath she wouldn't *choose* to agree to in order to see her father again. She justifies her action by quoting More's view about 'thoughts of the heart' and 'words of the mouth' (p.83), but More argues that the words of an oath have special value.

Consider how More values the oath Rich takes in Court (p.93), the standard legal 'swearing-in' formula still in use. Rich sets no value on the religious or ethical power of these words to bind him to be truthful.

In contrast, More explains what the real meaning of taking an oath should be. He demonstrates first to Norfolk (discussing the value of his oath of obedience to the King, p.53) and then to Alice (asking her to think about the meaning of taking an oath on the Bible, p.56) that an oath is a principled act that can't be broken or contradicted by honest people.

The desire for a simple life

Key quotes

'Ah, music! Music! Send them back without me, Thomas; I will live here in Chelsea and make music.' (Henry, p.33)

'I'm a plain simple man and just want to keep out of trouble.' ... 'Oh, Sweet Jesus! These plain, simple, men!' (The Jailer and More, p.88)

Bolt's play follows historical records in showing More's life pattern in Chelsea to be comfortable but relatively simple for a statesman, and framed by liberal humanist Christian values and practices.

The play picks up this idea first in Henry's sentimental yearning for More's garden and music-making away from troubles of the court. Indeed, he fantasises about a life of quiet ease in More's garden. This 'regret for Court life' is an ancient idea going back to Classical literature, where the weary ruler imagines escaping to live with a clear conscience in harmony with nature.

Obviously, Henry's dream is a passing fancy of an intelligent fretful mind with almost unlimited freedom to act. His material reality is framed by careful artifice (like the cloth of gold pilot's suit) and personal whim (deciding to leave before the laboriously prepared 'surprise' supper).

The idea is explored more thoroughly in the Common Man's desire for an uncomplicated life without responsibility, in whatever role he is being asked to play. He uses cunning and a show of fake ignorance to preserve a simple life because he's too lazy and self-centred to risk getting involved in anything that might require him to have an opinion or take a stand on an issue – which might lead to trouble. He's untroubled by conscience because he doesn't look further than the job.

More's outcry against 'plain, simple, men' (p.88) makes us think about the way people may hide behind 'timidity' as an excuse, like the Common Man as the Jailer. In various roles he demonstrates aspects of excuses we all recognise: indolence (can't be bothered), lack of concern (not my problem), pretending not to understand, having to go by the book, 'just doing my duty, sir' and so on.

DIFFERENT INTERPRETATIONS

Given the unconventional scene structure and Brechtian framing of the play, Bolt has already given us some freedom to think around issues and speculate on the meaning of the play's events from different character positions. More is the central character but he's constantly involved in a debate that tests his views – and you may not share his religious belief or agree with his behaviour. It is not possible to interpret the play's words any way we like because Bolt's characters are written to be more or less attractive to an audience in the way they express ideas. Nevertheless, we can open the play's issues to general debate.

Character perspectives

Think about the following questions to help you 'view' the play from the perspectives of the various characters. Each perspective allows you to 'read' the play in a slightly different way.

- If the Common Man were to be removed from the play, how might we view the action differently?
- What is Cromwell's pragmatic point of view? Where, for him, has More made fundamental mistakes about living in a state? Does Cromwell present a reasonable or convincing viewpoint at any stage?
- How has Cranmer squared his conscience as Archbishop of Canterbury and servant of the state?
- You could also consider the viewpoints of Norfolk, Margaret, Alice Roper, Rich and Henry. Each sees More's situation from a personal perspective in Bolt's play. How do the women's perspectives differ from those of the men?

Alternative endings

Consider how the two endings Bolt wrote offer slightly different interpretations of the action. Describe the different messages each ending sends about the play's events. Does the original ending suggest that these events are more ambiguous than the other? Does the Common Man's ending place greater emphasis on the relevance of these historical events to contemporary society? Imagine another ending you might write to represent your interpretation of the material.

What's right versus what's legal

More makes the assumption that the law is always going to enable an individual to live in safety. In his mind, the law will uphold ethical principles.

However, if we look at More from a Machiavellian perspective, we could argue that, despite being an intelligent and powerful man, he does things that make him vulnerable. Does he have an overly naive view that fails to recognise that the law is inevitably a product and an instrument of human beings? Should we pity More – or does he simply receive the fate that he chooses for himself by not acting in a more calculating and pragmatic manner?

QUESTIONS & ANSWERS

This section focuses on your own analytical writing on the text, and gives you strategies for producing high-quality responses in your coursework and exam essays.

Essay topics

1. 'Although More is the play's hero, the Common Man is really the "man for all seasons".' Discuss.
2. 'Norfolk remains a friend to More up to his death.' Discuss.
3. 'Although More is the head of his family, Margaret and Alice are free to express their own ideas.' Discuss.
4. Does the play show More's failings as well as his virtues?
5. 'Cromwell attacks More for using "conscience" as a defence because he knows he has sacrificed his own to "administrative convenience".' Do you agree?
6. '*A Man for All Seasons* demonstrates that it is wiser to adjust to the historical situation than to maintain conflicting ideals.' Discuss.
7. '*A Man for All Seasons* illustrates that ordinary people's lives are inevitably controlled by the will of leaders.' Do you agree?
8. "Better a live rat than a dead lion." 'The play suggests that some kinds of behaviour give you a better chance of survival than others.' Discuss.
9. 'The play demonstrates that in the end everybody has their price.' Do you agree?
10. '*A Man for All Seasons* shows that when those in power abandon their values, self-interest brings more success than integrity.' Discuss.

Analysing a sample topic

'The play demonstrates that in the end everybody has their price.' Do you agree?

The proposition asks you to consider 'everybody', and that includes More – so it's asking you to think beyond material rewards that a character like Rich is after. Rich will still be an essential part of your discussion but More is someone you might have been tempted to leave out of such an argument. Your opening paragraph should indicate that you realise More must be included.

A good place to begin your discussion is Rich's argument with More in the opening scene, because he states Machiavelli's proposition (that everyone has their price) – which More flatly rejects. Ask yourself why, and comment on Rich's idea that 'there's always something' a person wants.

Develop your discussion by showing how Cromwell tests and refines Rich's idea in their exchange at 'The Loyal Subject' – where Rich comes up with a personal definition: 'it would depend what I was offered' (p.43). Cromwell's following speech on 'rewards and penalties' leads Rich to understand the subtlety of gaining things in the world of public service.

Rich finally knows his price when he asks to be made Attorney-General for Wales (p.81) – although he seems to ask at an inopportune time, a 'price' will be agreed with Cromwell who needs Rich to commit perjury.

Go on to argue that More sees this 'price' as Rich's soul (p.95). Then contrast More's view with how other people in the play make compromises, find their 'price' – it isn't just Rich, although he's the most obvious crawler. Briefly select a couple from Wolsey, Cranmer, Cromwell, Norfolk, Henry, Alice and Chapuys; stress that some of them genuinely believe that the state must be served first.

Then come back to More for the final paragraph. You could argue in either of two ways:

- Does he have a price? If so, to do what? He hints that suffering might have an attraction (p.2). What would his religion have to offer More in order for him to do what he believes God wants him to do? You could argue that the world offers him his price – the chance to die for his belief.
- Alternatively, you could argue that More alone is not compromised, and does not have a 'price' in the way Rich (and Machiavelli) mean it to be understood. Arguing this way means ultimately disagreeing with the contention.

SAMPLE ANSWER

'*A Man for All Seasons* shows that when those in power abandon their values, self-interest brings more success than integrity.' Discuss.

In *A Man for All Seasons,* those who gain political power display great skill and understanding of their situation; they also show no hesitation in abandoning the values of justice and loyalty. Cromwell and Rich are inherently corrupt since they are entirely willing to regard truth and the law as malleable and flexible, able to be bent to their own will or the will of their ultimate master, the King. This in turn ensures that there is no protection for those like More, whose commitment to religious and legal principles places him at odds with the King's wishes. As the play unfolds, it becomes increasingly clear that a person of such integrity has no chance of success when those in power are ruled purely by self-interest.

The issue of corruption is raised in the opening scene, partly through Rich's line 'every man has his price' – suggesting that values can always be dispensed with for personal gain – and partly through More's story about the silver cup. This was an attempted bribe, but More is clearly not able to be tempted in this way: as Norfolk later asserts, More 'was the only judge since Cato who *didn't* accept bribes'. Rich, on the other hand, is quite willing to accept a bribe, or to enter into any deal that will advance his status. He begins the play unemployed and directionless; by its end he is 'Sir Richard Rich', Attorney-General for Wales and on his way to becoming a Baron and Lord Chancellor.

The extent to which Rich has abandoned his values is evident in his act of perjury, which effectively condemns More to death. His willingness to lie under oath not only regards the truth as a disposable commodity; it also causes a great injustice, since More has not actually committed the act of treason. Initially More tried to help Rich, recommending that he accept the Dean of St Paul's offer of a teaching job. However, far from expressing any sense of gratitude or loyalty to More, Rich 'repays' him by corrupting every principle More holds and stands for.

Cromwell is a mentor to Rich, and demonstrates all the qualities required for success in their society. For Cromwell it is less a question of material rewards than of successful service to King and country, but he carries out this service with a complete lack of attachment to any moral code or principle. He tells Rich to 'get sure' that he is 'not religious' and emphasises the practical notion of 'administrative convenience' over any abstract value. Thus, his conflict with More is a clash not just of personalities, but of philosophies: of convenience versus conscience, self-interest opposed to personal integrity. Indeed, More can see precisely the situation he is in – a world in which 'avarice, anger, envy, pride … commonly profit far beyond humility, chastity, fortitude, justice and thought'. It is a world, that is, in which Cromwell and Rich thrive, and More is ruthlessly eliminated.

More emerges as a man of great personal integrity, refusing to bend his beliefs even to save his own life. Yet he lives in a society where power is in the hands of those determined to succeed at any cost, and who have dispensed with values in order to advance their own status. Success in such a world requires the jettisoning of moral principles, of justice and truthfulness – of all the values, that is, that bind society together and give life a deeper sense of meaning and purpose.

REFERENCES & READING

Text

Bolt, Robert 1970, *A Man for All Seasons*, Heinemann, Oxford. First published 1960.

References

Chambers, RW 1935, *Thomas More*, Jonathan Cape, London.

Dickens, AG 1964, *The English Reformation*, Collins, London.

Fox, A 1982, *Thomas More. History and Providence*, Blackwell, Oxford.

Hall, N 2003, *Holbein's Conversation Piece – Sir Thomas More and Family*, published and distributed by Noeline Hall, PO Box 790, Robina, Queensland.

Kenny, A. 1983, *Thomas More*, Past Masters Series, Oxford University Press, Oxford.
Has a useful succinct discussion of More in Bolt's play in Chapter 7, pp.91–104.

Langdon, Helen 1986, *Holbein*, Phaidon Press, Oxford.

Machiavelli, Niccolo 1961, *The Prince*, trans. G Bull, Penguin, Harmondsworth. First published 1513.

More, Thomas 1965, *Utopia*, trans. P Turner, Penguin, Harmondsworth. First published 1516.

Wilson, Derek 2001, *In the Lion's Court*, T Marin's Press, New York.

Video

A Man for All Seasons 1966, dir. Fred Zinnemann, RCA/Columbia/ Hoyt's Video. Starring Paul Scofield (More), Leo McKern (Cromwell) and Orson Welles (Wolsey).

Websites

www.apostles.com/lastlett.html
Thomas More's last letter, written to his daughter, Margaret.

www.apostles.com/words.html
Words and phrases introduced into written English by Thomas More.

news.bbc.co.uk/2/hi/uk_news/946718.stm
What today's politicians can learn from Thomas More.

www.fordham.edu/halsall/mod/16Croper-more.html
William Roper's 'The Life of Sir Thomas More'.

www.historyguide.org/earlymod/stmore.html
A brief account of More's life and a description of More by his friend, Erasmus.

www.thomasmorestudies.org
Contains a wide range of material on More's life and work.